FLAWED *but* FABULOUS

Embracing a Better You

Michelle Best

CLAY BRIDGES
P R E S S

Flawed but Fabulous
Embracing a Better You

Published by Clay Bridges in Houston, TX
www.ClayBridgesPress.com

Scripture quotations are taken from the King James Version (KJV): King James Version, public domain.

ISBN: 978-1-7352217-7-9
eISBN: 978-1-7352217-8-6

To all my loved ones present and past who pushed me to be a better me.

To my dad, my pastor, and my circle, I wouldn't have been able to complete this without your speaking into my life. Love always.

Two months before she passed, I received these words in my birthday card.

The true essence of expressions could not be found in a card this year.
All that means is I'll just put pen to paper. You have proven, not because
you had to, just how much you've grown. How your heart has always
been in the right place. You work hard. You love harder. You give
sometimes until you've given out. My prayer for you, baby girl,
is this . . . Lord, cause my daughter to succeed on every level.
May she always shine and prosper in everything her hands touch.
Cause her happiness to be guarded and protected.
Jesus, continue to be the center of everything she does for
all the days of her life. . . . Love, Mom

TABLE OF CONTENTS

CHAPTER 1

FROM THE HEART

Inever imagined I would pen my life experiences to help others. My inner circle knows the anxiety I've faced and preference to just keep it all to myself. Let's just say it's a new day. In one way, it can be empowering yet a catch-22 to be so transparent. Life's journey can be filled with bumps and bruises.

This journey is teaching me that it's not about magnifying what happened but capitalizing on what's next. History is full of inventors who successfully failed, but their ultimate triumph is more popular. Part of my struggle stemmed from what happens next. Fearful about acceptance and rejection was a constant struggle until my prayer partner encouraged me to operate in faith over my fear. My prayer is that this deposit will begin a journey for people to see that the love of Christ can be found in any tragedy. Most important, whatever challenges readers find themselves in currently, there is another path to victory. Many of my prior challenges were magnified with embarrassment. I often intended that I would choose to carry them with me to my grave. One day, after an emotional high and low, I pulled out a journal and began to write to myself. I put myself in a posture that if someone came to me with the severity and concerns I carried internally, how could I help them?

SELF-REFLECTION

1. What is an experience you've dealt with that can be challenging to talk about?

_____

_____

_____

_____

2. Considering that experience, what were your initial thoughts about how it made you feel?

_____

_____

_____

_____

3. Related to that experience, what is something you would have done differently, given the chance?

_____

_____

_____

_____

CHAPTER 2

CAPACITY MATTERS

God is an awesome God who desires for us to be made complete. Sometimes, the scars of life will have us fake it until we make it. Everything in life happens for a reason. Scripture reminds the believer that "to everything there is a season" (Eccles. 3:1). *You are not what you experienced.* The most important thing you can remember is to use your experiences as opportunities to learn from them. Embrace the better you by building off your experiences. Maybe you planned on completing your education, but the credit hours and grades did not work out. Or perhaps you have been trying for a position with your company and cannot seem to get the yes you have been waiting for. Did you know that the last no does not mean no forever? There are countless professionals who will share their stories of repeated failures before they got it right. The point is that even if it does not work out the first time, that is no excuse to quit. Let me challenge the better in you by saying this: it is okay to try again. I recall some years ago having to remind myself of that same truth. My cooking journey has been eventful. I grew up watching my grandma in the kitchen, and everything was from scratch. Fast-forward to my day, and we like an easier button sometimes. Before I matured in the kitchen, I made a few dreadful blunders. Baking a cake is not meant to be challenging, so I thought. Yes, to all the bakers, it was a box of mix. The simple thing to do was follow the instructions on the box and it would come out looking just like the picture on the front. Wrong answer. What is advertised will not always be your experience, and guess what. It's okay. My first stab at baking a cake was a disaster. It wasn't because I didn't follow the instructions, but it did not work out as planned. After mixing and stirring, I poured my mix into the pan and placed it into the preheated oven. The next step was all about waiting for the final product. Long story short, no one told me not to put all the mix into one pan. I did not account for the expansion of the mix into a cake. My oven was full of cake mix that overflowed. Ironically, the batter kept trying to do what its purpose was under the heat of the oven, but my pan was unable to handle the capacity of my batter. The amount of batter was better suited for a standard bundt pan or two flat cake pans filled halfway. Based on my experience, I had several choices: give it up, just buy a cake, or get feedback to find out what I did wrong and try again. My experience was several years ago. Today, yours truly knows how to bake a cake from scratch. The point is that this did not happen overnight but over the course of time.

Know your capacity—operating beyond your capacity will lead to several unintentional blunders.

SELF-REFLECTION

1. Have you ever tried to do things beyond your capacity—handle more than you could? If so, how did you handle feeling over capacity?

    _____

    _____

    _____

    _____

    _____

2. Identify an experience you had that wasn't a failure but makes you laugh today.

    _____

    _____

    _____

    _____

    _____

3. Considering that funny experience, what did you learn from it?

    _____

    _____

    _____

    _____

    _____

CHAPTER 3

DEAL WITH IT

Avoidance Doesn't Heal

Transparency moment: I have this human internal mechanism of avoidance. This is not a good pattern, but I will share how I was able to break the cycle in my life. Avoidance says, "If I don't talk about it, it will resolve itself." If I avoid it, then I can get delivered. If you learn anything from my testimony, learn that avoidance is not deliverance. I have had a lot of painful experiences, some more embarrassing than others. The point is that acting like nothing happened isn't healthy. Maybe you've found yourself doing the same thing. Do you really feel better by not acknowledging it? Let me help you—*you don't feel better;* you've just learned a coping mechanism like anesthesia. My first method of defense was always to just avoid it. I did not care to talk or think about it. My internal defense had me thinking I was doing the right thing. Who wants to dwell on painful memories? Some things in life are beyond our control, while others may be a result of our decisions. Avoiding your issue or situation allows it to gain greater strength. Point: don't ignore the warning signs. During the first quarter of 2020, I found myself physically sick. In all my years of life, never had I had that type of feeling of an immediate pain level from 0 to 100 in a millisecond. After the embarrassment of waiting on an EMT to assess my need to be immediately transported to the local hospital, I decided to tough it out. First thing the following day, I was able to follow up with my primary physician who immediately knew the issue. Long story short, I had to have a procedure requiring anesthesia. I remember the anesthesiologist telling me she was injecting me with a little something to start the process. The next step would be a mask to cover my face, followed by a countdown until dreamland. Well, let's just say the last thing I remember is the nurse injecting me. I didn't need to count down. I slept very well through the entire procedure. My next memory was of being awakened. As lovely and pain-free as the anesthesia made me, it did not mean I would remain in that state. My procedure hurt like crazy, but it was necessary to make me eventually feel better.

Help Is a Good Thing

> *Two are better than one; because they have a good reward for their labour. For if they fall, the one will lift up his fellow: but woe to him that is alone when he falleth; for he hath not another to help him up.*
> —Eccles. 4:9–10

What happens when you ignore the flaw? I am so glad you asked. Ignoring the flaw creates a habitat for growth. One afternoon while driving down the interstate, I heard a clickity type sound. I was not sure what it was, but the noise was abnormal. The next day, I realized that the noise I heard was a small hair fracture crack in my windshield. It was not even comparable to a dime, so to me, that was minimal, and all was well. Learn from my mistakes. Do not ignore the flaw because it will have a way of getting your attention. Several months later, the weather changed to a cruel cold, colder than normal. My attention was no longer on the small crack because it did not appear to be growing, but then I needed to turn on my defroster. My assumption is that the change in temperature disrupted the flaw, causing it to expand. No longer was the sound small and distinct; it was a loud crack. Yes, I heard the sound and saw it with my own eyes. That small thing grew from smaller than a pin to more than half my window. The truth of this story hinges on the principle that my small flaw in my window was manageable until I ignored it and allowed it to grow. What personal character issues or flaws do you know you need to do better with but you love to convince yourself that "this is just me"? It is a good day to change that behavior to become a better you. You are more than your flaw, so why not start today to work on you to make you a better you. You are your own brand. What are you advertising? Trust me, somebody is always looking when you least expect it. Do not let them down. There is a better version in you.

Avoidance does not mean deliverance—it
means you delay your healing.

SELF-REFLECTION

1. Have you ever tried to ignore an issue but it just seems to never go away? Write down your thoughts.

    _____

    _____

    _____

    _____

    _____

2. Identify why the experience made you feel that way.

    _____

    _____

    _____

    _____

    _____

3. Is there another way to look at it or another perspective about what you ignored?

    _____

    _____

    _____

    _____

    _____

CHAPTER 4

ACKNOWLEDGE YOUR ISSUE

W hen is the last time you had a candid conversation—not the mediocre things but the real deal to look at the real you? Several months back, I had no choice but to look at where I was. Life will teach you to be fearful when you are accustomed to being a strong person. It can become intimidating to ask for help. Let me encourage you—don't be afraid to look at yourself, your true self, the real you, when no one is looking and judging you. You will only find solace at that moment when you no longer fear the you but embrace the you. I was encouraged to face my fear by one simple statement from my pastor's message. He reminded me to *be comfortable with your own voice again.* Those who are most familiar are aware how much I have loved to sing since I was very young. My youngest years began with a family group of cousins known as the Bestettes. My late uncle Lester "Nute" started the group with his children, and somehow, I ended up there. I know it's because he saw me as his daughter, but memory fails me how it all started. I only remember our matching outfits and tambourines. That's not the voice I'd grown uncomfortable with. It was my inner voice that reminded me of who I am. I am reminded of a passage of scripture involving David. After a battle, David and his men returned home to find that their wives and children had been taken captive. According to 1 Samuel 30:6, David encouraged himself. When is the last time you gave yourself a pep talk? I had always learned to pour into others more than I poured into myself. It should never be easier to encourage others while you neglect yourself. When you can't find the friend, counselor, pastor, or whoever you consider your right hand, you must have an in-the-meantime plan—do it yourself. What am I trying to say? We are all imperfect people full of flaws, but you cannot afford to dwell on them. The first step is acknowledging them so you can move beyond them.

Shabarbara, me, Tracey, Niecey

SELF-REFLECTION

1. Do you find it easy to admit when you make a mistake?

_____

_____

_____

_____

_____

2. Do you feel pressured to be perfect?

_____

_____

_____

_____

3. Name at least one area (flaw) you would love to change, and then list why you need to change it.

_____

_____

_____

_____

_____

CHAPTER 5

SCARED? FEAR OR FAITH—PICK ONE

For God hath not given us the spirit of fear; but of power,
and of love, and of a sound mind.

—2 Tim. 1:7

Whoever said fear can make you better? Yes, it sure can when you gain power to overcome it. My journey to writing began as a lamenting recommendation from my therapist. Yes, talking to a therapist—what in the world? No, seriously, sidebar—it is okay to talk to someone stronger than yourself. My life experiences have taught me that I can't always handle things on my own. Life can be a bit of a pickle, but it helps when you have a small, selective circle who can hear your heart without judgment. If you are in my small, exclusive circle, thanks. I know I've said it a million times and will continue to recycle my appreciation. I have a huge fear of failure. No, I'm not a perfectionist, but I just don't like to fail. When I put my hands to a thing, it's my intent to give it all I have. Anything beneath that isn't generally my standard. Although these guidelines have been my guardrails in life, it was this same thought pattern that prepared me for some huge downfalls. When I started to pen my thoughts, I decided to share them with my prayer warrior friend. Immediately, she saw more in my lament than I did. She felt people needed to hear it and be blessed, while I didn't see it that way. These are my private thoughts, victories, and failures. Who would even care? Honestly, I know she meant well, but I thought she missed it on that one. Several months later, I was unable to shake the idea, and here I am faced with a fear-or-faith decision. Fear tells me to stay within my bubble and keep it to myself, while faith tells me I've got a valuable voice of encouragement meant to help somebody. Fear told me tons of negative information about what people would think; meanwhile, faith was fighting just as hard for me. Fear will only grow while you feed it. I've learned that fear is fed best through my thoughts and affirmation. The key to conquering fear is by flipping the script on it, by feeding your faith to starve out the fear. Fear will try to display itself anytime you try to do something good or different. Fear says do nothing with the fabulous, but the better in you keeps trying to provoke you to do more. Never become stagnant and settled where you are. It is okay to want more. Fear will tell you not to try again because last time was a failure. Faith tells me that God will be with me regardless of how many times I fall or fail to accomplish my goals. Believe it or not, I was fearful of going to college as an adult student. I wished I had kept with my original plan to follow the typical path of college after high school and be done with it. My life didn't work that way. I was able to complete my associate's degree but immediately needed to enter the workforce. Working full-time and attending college is not an easy task. For several years, my fear of failing my courses kept me from trying to attend the local university. It took me several years to complete my bachelor's degree, but the joy I felt from accomplishing it was immeasurable. Thank you, University of North Carolina at Greensboro (UNCG); Spartans for life. Here's another long story, fast-forwarding some more years. I was back in college. Something in my psyche had said, do this to expand your portfolio at work and become more marketable for promotion. My speech sounded good until it was time to put in the work. Fear once again settled in that

I was way in over my head. During my last semester, less than three credit hours from completing my master's degree, the love of my life took ill. Fear had a new level—not only did it take over my ability to complete my assignments, but I also feared what my life would be like without my Sunshine, as I called her. My grandma has been my number-one supporter all my life, from birth even to now. Her physical absence doesn't decrease my drive because I know she's watching over me. I recycle all the encouraging words she spoke over my life. Grandma prayed me through my darkest times, so to run away and quit would have been an insult to all she had invested in me. My greatest fear became a reality on Thursday, December 12, 2019, as she took her final breath and I wasn't in the room physically

Grandma & me

with her. My heart is still broken, and I still grieve her loss. I know only God can heal me. I have good and bad days, but I'm no longer living in fear because Grandma would expect better of me. Second Timothy 1:7 reminds me that the spirit of fear isn't from God. I'm more encouraged by the latter part of the verse because the focus is on what God does give me. Instead of fear, I have power, love, and a sound mind. Guess what! That promise isn't just for me. This is a promise we should rehearse and meditate on daily. Being a better person is sustained by realizing you have power, love, and a sound mind. Giving in to the spirit of fear strips you or manipulates you out of having power, love, and a sound mind. Think about your last encounter with fear. Which of these areas was being attacked? Fear is so smart, but we know fear's method, so we can do better now that we know better.

SELF-REFLECTION

1. Name one of your biggest fears.

    _____

    _____

    _____

2. Based on the fear you listed, how would you handle the situation
    if your biggest fear occurred?

    _____

    _____

    _____

3. Find scripture(s) to support having faith opposite the fear driv-
    ing your situation.

    _____

    _____

    _____

4. Make the scripture(s) you listed part of your daily affirmation.
    List your affirmations below as a reminder when you are faced
    with fearful situations.

    _____

    _____

    _____

CHAPTER 6

WHAT YOU EXPERIENCED DOESN'T DEFINE YOU BUT REFINES YOU

In my career, I've had the opportunity to hold positions that have included fast-food worker, receptionist, bank teller, customer service, and management. Working in different positions was never an issue for me until I decided I wanted more. Fear will teach you to stay comfortable with your daily routine, although you know you want to venture out into something different. Wanting more sounds like a good thing until you don't get what you want. I literally applied for five positions I knew I was more than qualified for. The first rejection or two didn't bother me because I had several options available. I was interviewed multiple times, but every time it seemed within reach, I received that dreadful communication saying thank you for your time, but you are no longer under consideration. Now, the first few times, I was confident in stating, "Oh well, it's their loss" or "Whatever." It didn't faze me because there were other opportunities. Each rejection, though, continued to eat at my confidence little by little. By the time I applied for more positions, I no longer even made it to an interview. It seemed like the rejections came immediately. I began to develop all kinds of conspiracy theories because it did not make sense for them not to want me. My résumé was impeccable; my tenure and skills were phenomenal. My annual reviews were on point. Somebody tell me I was not being punked. The season of rejections from promotions was very challenging for me. I remember trying to find scriptural comfort in why the promotions that came from the east and the west did not knock at my door. There was part of me who wanted to give up totally and just accept that I would not be moving within the company. Before I could become content staying stuck, one of my prayer warrior friends randomly reached out with an encouraging message: "Go after it again." My initial response was "Girl, bye!" I thought that within myself because I dislike rejection. I was so over wasting my time. The very next week, my pastor preached the same sermon with points saying to go after it. Okay, Mr. Jesus, are you talking to me, or is that for Sis. Such and Such? Side note: Nothing in life is going to just knock at your door. Opportunities exist when you pursue them. So once I blew out the woe-is-me candle, I went at it again—strategically looking at positions within my caliber. I knew I could do it, and God was going to open the door. I just didn't know when. During the transition of waiting for my turn, I was inclined to pursue personal development courses to expand my portfolio. This was pivotal for me, and it will be for you. Rejection feels like failure, but it's all in how you look at it.

SELF-REFLECTION

1. Name a recent failure.

_____

_____

_____

_____

2. Based on the failure you listed, how did you initially handle the situation?

_____

_____

_____

_____

_____

_____

3. After reflecting, if this happened again, is there anything you would do differently?

_____

_____

_____

_____

_____

CHAPTER 7

BE A FINISHER

C an you really do this? Repeat with me: "Yes, I can." Sometimes we need a cheerleader. If you have a circle, praise Jesus for it. However, if you do not, you have to build your own. Turn on those creative juices, and do what needs to be done to be your team of one, if you must. Remember, we looked at David's decision to encourage himself. This situation created the opportunity for him to be better. Your issue, your failure, your flaw is creating the platform for you to be better. David was impacted in the same manner as the men, but the men blamed him as well. Self-reflection: don't allow what has happened to you to become your excuse to quit. Do you know how many times it took for me to get lost directionally before I finally learned the way? Several times I've found myself talking to my cousin on the phone while directions are being given from my GPS phone application. Sometimes, I would still miss my exit or misinterpret the instructions provided— don't judge me, it's a flaw. Hilariously, I would always blame the person I was speaking with for making me miss it. I can continue to waste time by staying in the wrong place, to point the blame, or to just simply acknowledge that I missed it and get back on track. Seriously, though, playing the blame game is nonproductive. At the end of the day, carrying the blame or inflicting the blame on others is a cop-out. It is easier to accuse the stronger person, but the mature person acknowledges their error and looks for resolve. Remember, in the beginning, we talked about the importance of owning your flaw. Now is not the time to curl up in a ball and never come out. You have a calling, a purpose on your life. Someone is waiting for you to break out of that dark place or the stuck place, as you call it. Nothing gets accomplished when you wallow in it. Yes, getting back up takes time. Don't invest more time in staying stuck than you do in momentum.

CHAPTER 8

FIX IT

When you notice something is out of order, do you tend to ignore it until later? Maybe you are that one friend who notices everything out of place—a microscopic pinch of lint or strand of hair—and just need to put it in its designated space. I'm always tickled with the animated memories of my grandmother. Side note: if you still have yours, love her to pieces; grandmothers are a treasure. Years before my grandmother passed, I had an uncle who lived in a facility because he needed more care than Grandma was able to provide at her age. My uncle had a roommate, and for the sake of this example, his name was Thomas. One day, Grandma was reading the obituaries and saw that Thomas XYZ had passed. Immediately, Grandma wanted to check on my uncle because Thomas had been his roommate at the facility for a while. On a visit into town, I drove Grandma to the facility. On the way back home, Grandma asked me if I remembered how she had said that Thomas had passed. I said yes, and she replied, "Well, I just saw Thomas in the room." My reply was, "Then he's not dead." We laughed for a few miles up the road. I recall asking Grandma how many people she told about that man's death. Now she had to call those same people to say Thomas wasn't dead. It was someone with the same name, wrong person. As comical as the story is, the life application is worth mentioning. When you mess something up, it's the responsible thing to clean it up. How many relationships have been ruined because of misinformation, and no one took the time to clean it up? I am often reminded of 1 Samuel 2:3 that says "by him [God] actions are weighed." This scripture carries a lot of weight about responsibility and accountability. Maturity says I am responsible for what I did, said, and thought. On the other hand, immaturity says it was never my fault, but I have a plethora of excuses to relieve myself of the truth. Taking the responsibility to fix your life does not negate anything you experienced, but the first step toward responsibility gives you an empowerment. You are valuable. You are worth it. You are better than anything that has ever happened to you.

I am also reminded of the scripture in Mark 2 when Jesus healed the man sick with palsy. During this incident, there was a group of friends willing to help their friend get to Jesus for healing. Sometimes, to get better, you must be transparent with God. What are you willing to release to get better? Ultimately, the press and exposure were built on faith, which led to the man's miraculous healing.

CHAPTER 9

FIND IT

By now, you've had some time to reflect on some flaws, failures, and fears. So what's next? You determine your next chapter. You determine your next story. If you are unsure, then it's okay to try to find it, but give yourself a deadline. When you are actively in pursuit of a thing, you conduct research. One day while getting ready, I told my niece who was three at the time to go get her shoes so we could go. It wasn't even three seconds when I heard her tiny voice. "Mimi" (yes, that's my nickname), "I can't find it." I responded, "Christie, did you look for it?" In her tiny voice, she responded again, "I can't find it. You find it, Mimi." Of course, when I entered her room, the shoes were sitting in plain view, and I replied, "Christie, did you look for it?" By that time, my presence encouraged her to find it. She finally realized I wasn't responsible for finding the shoes she took off and put in the closet. With joy, the tiny voice said, "I found it." In adulthood, it works the same way. Oftentimes, and I am being as transparent as possible, we want that easy button. It is easier when people do it for us. It is easier when it takes no energy or thought of our own, but is that really what is best for us? You will have a greater appreciation, just as my niece did, when you find it. Find your "it." What is your passion? What is your purpose? If you are still unsure, there are tools and resources that can help guide you, but the decision is yours.

What do you need to find to be a better you? Find it. Finding a passion may be a challenge to some and easier for others. Your next is whatever you want it to be.

And we know that all things work together for good to them that love God, to them who are the called according to his purpose.

—Rom. 8:28

Nay, in all these things we are more than conquerors through him that loved us.

—Rom. 8:37

To sum it all up, I am better today than I was yesterday. It's okay to remind yourself of the past, but it's never a good idea to wallow in it. Life happens and will continue to happen. You have the opportunity to make it better by the choices you make. Are you perfect? No, of course not, but with every victory, challenge, or failure, remind yourself that you are never alone. No more trying to be the Lone Ranger to tackle life's hardest hits by yourself.

REFLECTION AND AFFIRMATION

When you have those days of feeling your flaw is getting the better of you, here are some words from scripture I rely on to make it better.

> *For I know the thoughts that I think toward you, saith the LORD, thoughts of peace, and not of evil, to give you an expected end.*
> —Jer. 29:11

> *Beloved, I wish above all things that thou mayest prosper and be in health, even as thy soul prospereth.*
> —3 John 1:2

> *I will praise thee; for I am fearfully and wonderfully made: marvellous are thy works; and that my soul knoweth right well.*
> —Ps. 139:14

> *My flesh and my heart faileth: but God is the strength of my heart, and my portion for ever.*
> —Ps. 73:26

> *He healeth the broken in heart, and bindeth up their wounds.*
> —Ps. 147:3

ABOUT THE AUTHOR

Michelle Best grew up in Rocky Mount, North Carolina, under the leadership of her grandfather, the late Bishop F. C. Barnes. She has worked in the health-care industry for more than 19 years and holds an MBA in project management. Currently, Michelle is a faithful member of Monument of Praise Ministries in High Point, North Carolina, under the leadership of Bishop Kevin A. Williams. She serves on the minister's staff and is a praise and worship leader and a member of the choir. She enjoys any activity she can find to do.